WHY?!

Go

Conservative

John A. Jensen

Foreword

Lick, Lick, Lick…

Yes, I am still licking my wounds after the 2012 elections. As a proud American and Conservative, I cannot imagine why we would continue down the same path as the last 4 years. But that being said, I love my Country and want to fight on, reach higher, and try to fix whatever it is that we did not do to 'Win' the next election.

So it takes looking at what we did, both good & bad.

Was it the message?

Was it the Messenger?

Was it "How" we delivered that message?

And most directly,

WHY didn't the Conservative Message resonate?

Did we convince people on

"WHY?! Go Conservative"

Pro Small Efficient Compassionate Government

The U.S. Government serves at the will of the people. It is our belief that a smaller Government represents best, and is necessary to do things we cannot do for ourselves, while the individual Citizen should be empowered, allowed, and encouraged to decide most things for themselves. It is our belief that all monies should be spent for the greatest impact for the common good, not wasted on pet projects, personal gains, and rewards for lobbying efforts. It is our belief that a compassionate Government is there for the people in a time of dire need or natural hazard, but fully expects the people to provide for themselves and benefit by their individual efforts. It is therefore concluded that a small, efficient, compassionate Government is one that does not overspend, does not over tax, does not hide its decisions, does not reward the few at the cost of the many, does not penalize the people for hardship beyond their control, yet stands both ready and willing to explain itself in full upon request or necessity.

In Business and Life, there is a saying- "Never Enough."

In a simple way, it sums up the pursuit of higher ground, of what we do not already have. Business is an easy example since you chase higher sales, reducing costs, increasing productivity, making more money. Those are the primary drivers of Success. Life takes us down a similar path as people want to make more money, reduce what they spend, get more enjoyment out of Life, and keep more of what they made at the end of it.

BUT- then there is Government. You know the ones we elect and pay- and who consistently disappoint us. They operate on a much different premise.

Government believes in more money as well (those come in the form of taxes, penalties, surcharges, fees at the Federal, State, Local level), NO concern over costs (as they spend money they did not earn and know they can raise more money anytime they want), have NO incentive to raise productivity (as they simply will hire more people to handle additional workloads they create), and have NO care about balancing their checkbook (since the money isn't theirs and, if unspent, it will be budgeted away- so unrestrained spending becomes a good thing as opposed to bad).

The Conservative mindset is simple. We believe in a Smaller, Efficient, and Compassionate Government. Sure- Government has a place. Its place is to do for us what we cannot do for ourselves, and then get out of the way. Literally.

IF we ran Government like a business we would want to increase sales (size of our Gross Domestic Product), lower costs (taxes on its people), raise productivity (making the most out of every tax dollar), and keeping more money in the hands of people who earn it- that means YOU, the American citizen and taxpayer.

The Government should protect us and keep us in check on the big issues, but let us have the Freedom to decide, create, move, purchase, and live as we choose. Period…

The Conservative mindset isn't that we don't care, it isn't that we are selfish, it isn't that we protect the rich, it isn't that we are for "whites only". In actuality- we are the only party to be so incredibly open to all walks of life, of all backgrounds, of all religious faiths, of all levels on the income scale.

The Constitution mentions Life, Liberty, and the Pursuit of Happiness.

IF you believe in those and you want your government to spend wisely and more productively, there is a Good Chance you have a big piece of Conservatism inside of you.

"Why?! Go Conservative" takes you through the Conservative Platform step-by-step with this in mind, that you will read it and then apply it to your daily life and what you expect from your Government. And that brings up this simple point.

The Government is hired and paid for by YOU- they work and serve you, not the other way around.

Pro Election Policy

The ability to vote is a Right (and should be encouraged in every way) for American citizens, so we need to challenge the integrity of the system on a recurring basis. We believe that Democrats and Independents should not influence our Primary outcomes. We believe that only current residents in legal standing should have the Vote- so all registers should be purged in non-election years to represent current accuracy. We believe that having a form of ID is necessary to register to vote, which means than one has an ID, and therefore should show that proof to validate the integrity of the vote when casting it.

Want to know some really sad statistics?

There are about 330,000,000 people in the United States.

The 2012 Election had about 127,000,000 people exercise their right to Vote.

Most people fall in to one of two camps- they either Vote religiously and seriously, or they Vote infrequently (possibly never) as "it never changes anything".

One of my ideas was to incentivize people to GO VOTE. What about a tax credit to exercise your vote or a tax penalty if you don't? Besides the fact I hate social engineering, I love the idea. Kind of a "Forced Patriotism" agenda.

But then I became the problem- since I just put Government in charge of something else and took away another freedom. Did you catch it?

You have the right to Vote. You have the right to NOT vote as well. That is a Freedom we have in this country. The ability to get into or away from our political system of choice. If we were to mandate voting, then the results would change. They wouldn't change for better or worse, they would change based on a FORCED outcome. Why would someone who doesn't want to Vote take it seriously or vote their conscience?

The flipside is also true. The more you invite Government (or it invites itself) into your Freedoms, the more it consumes of you and your life, the less choice you will have, the more forced the outcome gets. Eventually- they control your World and your life (ability to choose) is over. Government is not the answer to problems, it IS the problem.

The Right to Vote is where Conservatism starts- you have Freedoms in this Country. Those are fought for during wars, debated over kitchen tables and in legislative halls, and defended by the ultimate warrior- YOU, the American citizen and taxpayer.

Conservatism is based on individual Liberty, States rights, and the belief that a smaller, efficient, compassionate Government needs to do some things we cannot do for ourselves, but then let us figure out the rest.

That is what the American Dream is based on- YOU can be anything you want.

It starts with the wonderful Freedom and Right to Vote, and those Elections need to be fair and just- and serve as our judgment on the work done by the Elected Officials that serve us.

Elections always have Consequences.

Remember that, and Choose Wisely.

Pro Effective Congressional Representation Policy

Congress should amend the Ethics Reform Act of 1989 to remove the automatic Cost of Living (COLA) pay increases for Congress. In order for Congress to initiate pay increase they must bring a Bill to the floor for a Super Majority vote and the pay increase will not take effect until the next Congress. All changes to Congressional pay or benefits must be posted on all Congressional websites and distributed through available media outlets for a time period of 30 days prior to any vote on the floor.

All voting records should be simplified and made publicly available via Congressional websites in a user friendly format. All bios for Congress should also include a copy of their parties Platform so citizens can be easily reminded where their loyalty and priorities are.

All matters of national significance or substantive change should be timed to allow to national public dissemination via public media outlets, town hall forums, and regional mailings. This should be a minimum of 30 days after the legislation has been written to allow to common public understanding and comment.

A government of the people, by the people and for the people should not be compromised by special interests, up to and including Public Unions. All communications and interactions should be publicly documented, and access balanced between formal lobbyist bodies and the Representatives true geographic individual constituents. All lobbyist and union efforts should be considered a "for profit" entity as the nature of their group is to represent the better financial well being of a small sect of the constituency.

If you ran a business, you would hire employees. Would you then pay them to do what they want, or do what you want? Think of your own job- do you do what you want or what your boss wants? There is a hierarchy to getting a job done- but first and foremost is knowing who answers to whom. That isn't negotiable, it is necessary. That our government is elected by us & paid for by us- means they WORK for us and are there to do what is in our collective best interest.

Is spending money we don't have in our best interest?

Is putting their job prospects and re-election over what needs to be done- in our best interest?

Is doing all of this in back rooms and without our knowledge in our best interest?

Is giving access to special interests with money in our best interests?

Is giving themselves a pay raise when we are in massive debt in our best interest?

IF your answer to these questions (and countless more) was "NO!", then you are definitely on the path to being a Conservative-in-Training, or maybe there already!

Pro Expansionary Economic Policy

The need for a strong dollar, liquid capital markets, high employment, pro-growth business regulatory policies, and continued development of the Middle Class cannot be sacrificed by the wasteful spending of a large Federal Gov't through deficit spending, high national debt, increases in tax revenues, and poor leadership.

We believe in a strong America-first principle which should reward domestic U.S. hiring, encourage repatriation of jobs and industries, create a business-friendly environment that makes companies choose to GROW U.S. on the merits, and celebrates the success of American innovation.

We believe strongly in rebuilding the Manufacturing sector of our economy. Our "manufacturing dependency" is viewed as a weakness, bordering on a national security risk. If we are to offshore all manufacturing, we become as susceptible to foreign manufacturing influence as energy dependence historically. Therefore, it is paramount to reform the tax code and regulations which burden manufacturing, without sabotaging our great nation's environment, and reintegrate manufacturing into the core of our economy.

The American dream usually takes on one of two forms- you want to start your own business or want to get promoted up the corporate ladder in someone else's business. No matter which path you take- you take it for a simple and common reason.

You want to have a better life, and provide a better life for your family.

Without a strong economy, BOTH of these dreams are over. There is no way to take the ultimate risk and succeed in a start up business when the economy stacks the deck against you, Government regulations and red tap choke up innovation, money isn't being loaned out by banks, demand isn't there for whatever idea you have, and the Risks far outweigh the Reward.

Same thing for being moved up the corporate ladder. How can you move up in a hiring freeze? You can't make more money when there isn't more money to pass around (unless you are in Government currently). How can you get that "next best job" when there is too much labor and not enough competition for talent and skills? Why would someone even keep you at a top salary you currently make if they can't justify the return on that investment?

We need a Strong Economy to make us ALL better off.

So now what makes a great economy?

It takes a strong dollar- since a weak dollar takes away purchasing power and literally causes you to lose money by the simply dilution of that currency.

What would cause a weak dollar?   Quantitative Easing by the Federal Reserve.

Think of it this way- the more money you print, the less each piece of paper is worth as its percentage of the economy. As you print money, you have to offset it with debt. IF you print too much money, it undermines the confidence people perceive in the ability to pay off that debt and reduces the exchange rate other countries will pay you. Our Credit rating (perception of ability to pay debt off) and exchange rate are critical to our domestic success.

It also takes liquid capital markets- since easy money allows for construction, large purchasing, new business investment or start ups, and others.

Banks need to be willing to loan and take some good risk.

People need to be willing to take out loans and bet they can grow a business.

Consumers need capital at fairly low rates to be able to pursue their happiness.

Confidence and Certainty are crucial bedrocks of building a strong economy.

High Tax rates, Burdensome Regulations, Big Government, & Bailouts all interfere in the Free Trade market place and interrupt the efficient system we call Capitalism.

It also takes High Levels of Employment- since this allows for upward pressure on labor rates, competition for skills and talent, encourages a positive work demeanor and spirit, and maximizes the levels of

Government revenue & money in the economy as discretionary spending of consumers.

It also takes a pro-growth regulatory environment- since this gets government out of the way and allows business to thrive. You want a perfect example?

Keystone Pipeline

The pipeline from Canada down to the Gulf would create over 100,000 jobs permanently and over 1 million jobs for the construction side of it. Environmental was a concern, until that was redesigned and approved. We are energy dependent and need to do everything we can to get ourselves more and more away from that, as it puts us potentially at a National Security risk or economic risk.

Yet the Pipeline Approval papers sit on someone's desk as we wait on job creation. We wait, even though the millions of people looking for a solid job would love to have an opportunity to work on the pipeline.

It also takes certain behaviors of Government to not put working folk at risk.

The Government cannot deficit spend as it is money we do not have, that puts future generations at risk. Would you overspend at your job? Would you overspend at your home- knowing full well you didn't have the income to pull it off, and would have to give that debt to your kids?

The Government cannot run a high national debt as it threatens our credit rating, which in turn increases the amount of interest we pay and makes other nations less inclined to invest in our Country.

The Government needing to increases tax revenues is another huge impediment to growth and expansionary policies. Any increase in tax revenue is money taken out of economic circulation, and also money less efficiently used.

All of these, amongst others, are examples of poor leadership in Government.

Ask yourself this-

When has Government done something better than the private sector?

Pro Energy Independence Policy

Led by private industry, we aim to make America energy independent in the near term. ALL aspects contributing to the domestic energy supply needs to be considered. All types such as Wind, Hydro power, Clean Coal technologies, Solar, Nuclear, Domestic and Offshore Oil drilling, Nat Gas, new forward looking technologies; and realistic, economically viable conservation programs are to be reasonably considered through the lenses of what can solve our independence for the future, provide energy in a cheap and reliable fashion, and be provided by the Private sector without (or with temporary and minimal) subsidies.

We believe that our Energy policy should be comprehensive and long term in nature. All aspects of energy should be developed and provided by the private sector, under the limited oversight of the Federal Gov't. As energy is critical to our economic prosperity, we believe it is critical that all aspects be investigated and developed to be protected from outside threat. One possibility is the regional development of Energy Parks on former or current military sights- this eliminates the "not in my backyard" argument, provide security, regional disperses Energy solutions, and provides for economy of scale in all necessary infrastructure required. These parks might be a Private/Public partnership or simply a leaseback/security provision relationship only.

We believe that any export of Energy needs to be Value Added Taxed to provide compensation for the tighter domestic supply that would create, as a trade off toward any temporary and minimal subsidies the Energy sector is supplied.

For generations, we have been at the mercy of foreign nations do to our energy dependence. We are a nation of Freedoms and capitalism. We are a nation priding itself on driver independence, and the ability to own a car, or maybe more.

We like the open road, and welcome the Freedom to travel this great land and see our friends, family, vacation, get to work, fly abroad, and more based on the affordability of oil and gas.

After 9/11 we realized we need to watch our backs regarding National Security. And when it comes to energy dependence, we teeter on the brink of economic threat every time this is a spark of turmoil in the Middle East. The price at the pump puts tremendous pressure on our economy via our consumer discretionary spending and margins at our place of employment.

Our energy dependence is an addiction we need to end. And the means is now here.

Recent technologies have allowed us to free previously unreachable natural gas and oil deposits which now puts America in a wonderful position of becoming energy independent <u>and even begin to export oil/natural gas.</u>

Conservatives always put "America First" and are proud to showcase our talents, our resources, and are wealth. It is not embarrassing that we are a land of riches, but should be celebrated. It should not be something we postpone, but something we invite and find ways to say "Yes We Can".

No amount of energy independence should come at the price of our planet, or our country. But Conservatives understand that the Greater Good needs to be served, so we don't look for excuses on why we shouldn't do things in life- we look for ways we can do them.

Safely putting America First, and getting us off Energy Dependence, is the first step in a greater Economy and bringing the American Dream back to life.

Pro Immigration Policy

The U.S. Government shall use all means under current Federal Law(s) to protect our borders in this day of International Terrorism as a priority and by all means necessary. The historical flow of illegal immigrants must be dealt with as we are a Rule of Law country. It is paramount that all our borders are secured completely to reduce the National Security threat, both from terrorism and illegal activities that currently operate uninhibited. The current illegal alien community needs to be converted in one of two ways 1) proud and reputable people should be provided a onetime path to citizenship, although probationary for first 5 years 2) non-reputable, or people with criminal/disruptive behaviors, need to be deported and not allowed to return. All companies must institute a Social Security check policy as formatted by Federal Gov't law and incorporated at the State level. Safe haven cities must become a thing of the past as it simply condones an illegal way of life within our Rule of Law nation, which is inherently unfair to the current pool of law abiding citizens. The level of legal immigration should be significantly increased, streamlined and targeted to encourage people of all walks of life, of all educational levels, and for continued success as a melting pot of cultures.

Racist. Yes, I said it. But I said it before you did so we can get this lunacy out of the way.

Conservative means Racist, right? Isn't it the White party? We're oppressive, right?

This is where I need to tell you to get a grip on yourself and wake up. Want some coffee? You know- to help you wake up to the Truth?

Think of it this way- which is more fair, open, and non-racist- the party who looks at all people equally and let's the most talented rise up, or the party that looks at color and race as a way of categorizing and putting quotas in place?

The Conservative party doesn't look at someone through a filter of what race, sex, age, religion, etc. We look at people as just that- PEOPLE. What they believe, how they act, what they say, what have they achieved- We start equal & let our actions take us into various opportunities. And ones actions and results, these are what people should be held accountable.

That Barrack Obama has dark skin doesn't concern me, that his Presidential policies are suffocating this nation's economy and culture concern me greatly. Does that make me a racist? No. It makes me an American who cares about his Country and its future.

Immigration is not about race. It is about solving a problem we have had in this Country since its inception, on all borders and through various methods.

After 9/11, our secure borders take on a much more meaningful tone. That we can live free from outside threat is a service Government needs to provide, as we cannot provide it for ourselves.

Pro Strong Defense Policy

We believe in a strong national defense, while understand there are numerous avenues of waste within the defense sector. These should be identified and eliminated over time, and always improved upon.

We believe that the U.S. military should allow military personnel to carry firearms while on base. The 1993 Clinton ban should be lifted so that soldiers can be prepared to defend themselves at any time. Especially given the Ft. Hood scenario and a heightened possibility of a spontaneous terror threat, this limitation is outdated and should be lifted.

We believe in an America First defense, which should allow us to consolidate foreign bases strategically and brings numerous soldiers home and out of harm's way, without sacrificing our nation's security interests.

We believe in a safe and secure presence overseas, so if decide to stay off-country, and then we need to evaluate each site on a case-by-case basis to insure the safety of our men and women abroad.

We believe in a strong national security policy- so any threat to that needs to be confronted in real time and any information challenging it needs to be communicated in an expedited time frame.

We need to re-evaluate all countries and relationships clearly to understand who our Ally is truly, who is an Enemy (threat), and who is neither. Our fiscal decisions via our national government or through other bodies (IMF, World Bank, U.N., etc) must be determined to not reward non-allies or provide monies for terror-related countries. Any ally must understand that standing with us has a reward, whereas standing against us has a price. All foreign relations decisions should immediately be reflected in Trading Partner status with that country.

The largest function of our Government, which all would agree is something we cannot do for ourselves, is Defense. Our country and freedoms are predicated on our safety, on trust, on certainty, and on the understanding that no other country or entity will threaten that lifestyle.

The Conservative message is a belief in a strong Defense. We need to have enough firepower to deter the offensive acts of others. We need enough soldiers, weapons, and breadth to respond to any global event. We need to be prepared domestically/internationally, in hard assets and intelligence, and in physical, diplomatic, & cyber units. The ability of someone to take down the United States as a Superpower, and as a beacon of Freedom in the world, cannot be allowed to happen.

We need to prioritize this. We need to fund this. We need to upgrade this.

We need to take care of the Men and Women who protect our Freedom.

Our international relations need to be thoroughly re-evaluated. What makes up an ally? What standards do we expect them to hold? What do we expect from them in exchange for being an Ally? What aid to we extend, and what is the price tag for that money?

In the end, you cannot have a weak defense and a strong country. It takes commitment, it takes money, and it takes a constant approach to updating our reach, evaluating our systems and efficiency, and protecting our freedoms in a way that does not impede the very liberties we are trying to protect.

Ask yourself a simple question:

IF you didn't have a strong defense and were threatened either by an outside country or terrorist group, who would step up and keep them from your doorstep?

Pro "American First" Trade Policy

International Free Trade is only good if all countries conduct such trade by the same rules. In the reality where Free Trade Agreement cannot be reached, then we need to pursue Fair Trade practices. At no time can we allow trade agreements to favor either nation or reward the off shoring of U.S. jobs.

The U.S. trade deficit sends much of America's wealth to foreign countries since many of them engage in unfair unilateral trade practices that include adding numerous Tariffs, Port of Entry Taxes and Import Duties on American products. Congress should enact laws that Reciprocates (Copies) those fees on products from each country that exports to the U.S. This will level the playing field since countries will then pay the same fees imposed on U.S. products.

We police the World. We keep running a trade deficit. We depend on other countries for energy. We export jobs, more than we export goods and services.

We uplift other countries and economies through Aid, IMF/World Bank investment.

And we do ALL of these usually at the detriment of our own Country.

Conservatives believe in America First. We are not alone on the planet, but we seem to take better care of others than of ourselves.

Why don't we build a great country and let others do that for themselves?

Why are we to sacrifice our Men and Women to protect those who won't stand up for themselves?

Why are we giving Aid to the very Countries that harbor and encourage terrorism which threatens our future?

Why are we buying goods from other countries and encouraging the offshoring of jobs, without leveling the field and competing for that business?

When was the last time you COULD truly "Buy American"?

The conservative view is not to be isolationist, but to be much more particular about why we get involved. The view is not to commit half-heartedly, but to be the last act of every story we need to be involved in. We have too many issues here at home, so that to provide this many international interventions for their gain and our loss are truly illogical and unwarranted. Why are we more concerned about other countries business and not about bring manufacturing home? Why are we more concerned about Democracy in other countries, when the Liberties here at home are slowly slipping away?

It is time to rethink our global strategy and truly place- AMERICA FIRST.

Pro Fiscal Restraint and Balanced Budget Policy

We believe in a Balanced Budget approach to Government. As our belief causes us to keep Government small and efficient, it also requires Congress to pass and enact a Balanced Budget annually, except in times of war or National emergency. Those exceptions should be included in budgets moving forward and are not exceptions after the first budget year.

We also believe that a recurring analysis of all monies spent is warranted to improve efficiencies over time. Our tax dollars need to be efficiently spent, minimized, and accounted for in a transparent fashion.

How can you spend more money than you have and stay in business?

How can you keep extending your own credit without the ability to pay it off?

These are simple questions, but truly get to the core of Conservatism. You need to make great decisions, act on those, and live with the outcome. Period. That you take on crazy risk knowing you will be bailed out or not taking care of yourself because you think Government to do it for you, these are as unacceptable as spending someone else's money wastefully and them enjoying you are doing it.

It doesn't make any sense, and it threatens every one of us.

If the United States does not get a grip on its financial future, we will all pay the ultimate price in the loss of liberties, loss of reserve currency status, loss of wealth, loss of trading advantage, and complete bankruptcy in one of several ways.

And understand this, there is no such thing as continuing on our current course and balancing our budget. There will be changes, reductions, eliminations, and enough restraint to make it felt by everyone in the Country.

Think about the visuals of people rioting in Greece because they couldn't keep everything that was promised to them, although they couldn't pay for it EVER.

Do you want that to be us?

That is the United States future unless we come together and make some real hard decisions collectively as a country. No one can keep everything they have. We all must understand the greater good of our Country, the future of Generations, and our complete financial existence is at stake.

One year at a time. One decision at a time.

By Substantive Acts, not Political Soundbite.

Pro U.S. Constitution, Bill of Rights, and faith in God

The U.S. Constitution and Bill of Rights are the Supreme Law of the land and shall be taken literally. Our rights are natural rights and are given to us by our Creator that no man can take away.

We believe in a small and non-intrusive Government, so the need to keep it simple and focused on the Constitution, Bill of Rights, and God is critical to our success. All other attempts at legislation are considered without foundations and standing, and therefore an attempt at overreach as opposed to a small, efficient, compassionate Government – no matter the issue it addresses or the method.

A small non-intrusive Government allows for money to stay in the hands of the person who made it, and allows them to spend it as they see fit. Does that sound like you?

The conservative view is to minimize government's involvement in our life, to increase the personal responsibility and reward for people's decisions in Life.

Go back when you were a kid- did you like when your parents told you to do something?

Of course not, no one did.

The greatest good for everyone is to grow a Country of proud Americans that want to stand on their own two feet, which want to pursue the American dream, that what to make their world better for their family and future generations, and that are accountable for their mistakes as well as celebrate their success.

Government does not build Business- Americans do.

That takes risk, money, attitude, faith, commitment, sacrifice, & a dream of a better life.

The Constitution, Bill of Rights, and the fiber stemming from our religious faiths are simply the starting points of the backbone in this nation, but they are also non-negotiable standards and guarantees which we are woven into the very fabric of America.

They are not distant relics we occasionally talk about, but the concrete foundations of Conservative values.

Pro Transparency

Important legislation can be written in comprehensive language, as the Declaration of Independence, Constitution and Bill of Rights clearly demonstrate. All Bills enacted by Congress must be written in plain, common-sense English prose that is comprehensive and understandable by citizens.

We believe in encouraging a national dialogue, involving the citizenry to comment, providing access and availability in this technological age, and insure proper timing for laws to be review before brought to the floor for vote.

If you want to talk-the-talk, then you should walk-the-walk.

I guess another way to say is our politicians should lead by example. When was the last time your politician truly made you proud every day? When was the last time you were disappointed in your political leader?

We spend too much time being disappointed & not enough time being proud.

The need for true Transparency in Government is critical to us changing that routine. We need to know what they are doing and changing, so we can hold them accountable to what our needs are.

Our leaders represent us. We Vote them into office, or out. They serve the taxpayers, the Electorate, the Citizens- people like you and me.

I don't think it's rational for anyone to expect their leaders to do everything they want and nothing that they don't like. Sometimes, we need compromise to get things done. There are moments the Country needs something that is against our philosophy.

Transparency is the difference maker. Our politicians should treat the American people like Adults, and tell us WHY they make decisions. They should bring us into the conversation, after all- isn't communication critical to a successful relationship?

Think about the Affordable HealthCare Act (Obamacare). It was written in the dark of night, behind closed doors, rushed to be voted on, read AFTER it was written, and never revealed to the people. Does that sound like the transparent government of true representation?

Where was the national dialog? Where were our leaders in explaining this to us? Where was the compromise and bipartisanship? Where was the Greater good vs. simply an egotistical and ideological victory?

How they do, What they do, THAT they do. It starts with transparency, trust, & respect.

Pro Equality Policy

We believe in a Merit based approach to our great nation- where no color, race, gender, age, disability, religion or any physical/ancestral quality should be included in the decision making process. We believe strongly that one's performance, work ethic, and personal advances should be singular in making decisions.

We believe in a level playing field, where all people are truly created and treated equal, and that is critical to our success as a broader nation. We believe that America is a wonderful melting pot of cultures which is to be celebrated and encouraged, not divided and penalized.

Equality of opportunity is a right, and the individual success in advancement from that point up to each citizen to achieve for him/her self. "We, the People" must stand united in our protection of the American dream where anyone can become successful, regardless of their origin or beliefs.

This is a pretty simple thought. Everyone is treated equally- period. They should never be discriminated against, nor given an unfair advantage. And that is where the difference is between parties and ideals.

One party wants to group everyone into smaller clusters and divvy out little pieces of success based on what race, religion, gender, or age makes up that smaller sect *without any concern for the achievement or talent behind it.*

Let me repeat that one- without any concern for the achievement or talent behind it.

The other party wants to group everyone together and then let people go thrive, achieve, earn, and receive their lot in life WITHOUT any concern toward what race, religion, gender, or age them makes up.

Let me restate that- without any concern for what race, religion, gender, or age.

Which is more equal- that which segregates and divides OR that which treats all equally and lets the victor keep the spoils?

Conservatives don't divide. Conservatives don't care what God gave you at birth, but only what you chose to do with yourself after being born.

Pro Taxpayer Policy

We believe in a pro-business environment, and through that, a pro-labor one. The American dream should not exclude or penalize anyone- nor should it unfairly reward/punish individuals in business. Companies need create an effective productive rewarding environment for their labor force. Labor needs to be rewarded within the framework of the company structure, without damaging the very company that rewards its productivity.

We believed in Labor- but strongly disagree with the need and/or current execution of Labor Unions. This applies to private and public- yet public take a different path as the revenues come from the taxpayer. As we believe in efficient use of Government funds, then Public unions (ones in Gov't) need to change or be eliminated. As we believe in merit being rewarded as opposed to any general "class" or people, the use of unions in Government reduces efficiency, dilutes productivity, and creates a restrictive labor force that is harmful and against the grain of a smaller, efficient Government that works for all people equally.

 A government of the people, by the people and for the people should not be compromised by special interests, up to and including Public Unions.

A government of the people, by the people should also not be threatened and responsible for the insurance of private company pension plans. If a Private Company wants to have a pension, that is their choice- but they need to account for, pay for, insure for implementation of that pension, without involvement or responsibility of Government.

One of the perks about a small, efficient government is that you get to be more the decision maker about where you money goes.

The only way to a smaller efficient Government is by getting the Lobbyists, Unions, & Special Interests out of the way.

They have a right to a voice EQUAL to the normal taxpayer, not above the taxpayer.

The taxpayer needs to come first. When was the last time you paid for something, but didn't have input into what you wanted for your money? When was the last time someone else had more control over your money than you did? The sad answer is every time you sent money to Federal, State, and Local Government.

It isn't that these entities aren't needed. It is simply they need to keep their focus on the only thing that matters-benefitting the American people.

Pro Life Policy

Human life is nature's continuum which begins at fertilization and is not interrupted until natural death. Constitutional personhood is the secular legal definition of the continuum of life. It is a law of logic that contradictory statements cannot be true at the same time. If nature's continuum of life is true, then the secular continuum of life must also be true because if the secular continuum of life contradicts nature's continuum of life, one is false.

Pro Traditional Marriage

We believe that true marriage is only between one man and one woman. We do not believe that same sex marriage should be publicly acknowledged by Government as it is against our strong Family Value platform. Support the current Defense of Marriage Act (DOMA) that allows any state to not recognize the same-sex marriage license issued by another state.

During the 2012 DNC, the Democrats were taking "God" out of the platform. When they tried to put "God" back in to it, there was a lot of Booing in the audience.

Do you believe in God? Do you believe in strong Family Values?

This is a key pillar of Conservatism, and one we celebrate- not avoid or chastise.

Our pro-life and pro-traditional marriage outlook isn't saying anything about individual rights or about the legality of such things, but based that God had intended Life to be lived based on traditional values.

It is not for others to decide- but more between you and your creator.

If you want to avoid, ignore, reduce, or Boo God- then be a Democrat.

If you include God, celebrate faith, and strengthen Families- Be Conservative.

Pro Global Leadership Policy

The U.S. takes a stronger leadership role in the United Nations and/or considers dissolving our self from it and removes the United Nations from American soil. It is not acceptable that the United Nations (or any world body) work against our America First format for national security. This should always be similarly true of any international body of which we are a part.

The United States has a proud history of involvement in Global issues. It is the largest participant in the IMF, World Bank, NATO, UN, and the last remaining superpower in the world.

We should never take this responsibility lightly, nor let this position be devalued by how we are treated or respected by other nations or bodies.

That we are the main source of funding behind initiatives should give us clout.
That we have national security concerns should never be belittled.
That other nations' understand clearly our stance on issues, and stand by us, should be without parallel.
That other nations' trade, supply or empathize with nations who stand against us should be challenged and resolved without fail.
That our Allies are not clear, and these unified bodies do not respond to our leadership, is both unfortunate and unacceptable.

These times dictate a need to prioritize national threats above all else. How can you continue as a nation of Free Trade and Liberties when outside threats might eliminate that very possibility?

Part of dealing with national threats is dealing with Allies (who are they and what shape do they take) and updating global affiliations. Why be a member of a body that will not take a firm and active stance with us in preserving our Country? Why do we continue to allow trade status upgrades to countries that are not responsive or inclusion to nations that do not respect their own citizens (let alone other nations of the world)?

We should not be isolationist- but we also must raise the bar on what we expect from our friends, and emphasize what we will not tolerate from our enemies.

Pro Public Accountability

We believe that our elected officials work for us, and should be held accountable for their actions- both credit and blame. There is no way to do this fairly without Transparency, and once you have that- then Accountability. Elected officials should know the platform for the Party that elected them and hold true to that for the most part, unless the greater national good is served by compromise in an exceptional sense.

Ever think we live in a world of intolerance? Ever see a "good leader" make a mistake and get publicly destroyed unfairly OR get a complete pass when having done something wrong?

Accountability is just that- the ability to hold our leaders accountable for their decisions.

That our leaders make solid, transparent decisions for the greater good of our nation is mandatory.
That they are perfect is unreasonable.

Conservatives don't want perfect leaders, but we do want leaders to lead by example, to be responsive to the public trust that elected them, to make decisions for our well-being more than the furthering their own career.

By serving the public well, you should be re-elected. By breaking the trust or not getting the results as best you might, you should be voted out of office.

Elections have Consequences.

So do the decisions and acts in your personal life, for better or worse.

Conservatives believe America is a Nation of Laws, and as such we need to hold each other accountable to that standard, whether they are Democrat or Republican, Independent or Conservative.
We don't look for ways to excuse bad behavior, but look for resolution of accountability without favoritism.

Conservatives do not get a pass, rather they represent the higher standard.

Pro Tax Reform

We believe in a simpler and more transparent tax code. Although the code must be progressive to take pressure off the less fortunate, it is our determination to make everyone pay something and therefore have a stake in their future. Success is not the enemy, but the goal in a capitalistic society. Our great nation of equality levels the playing field for success, but it is a burden of the wealthy, in part, to help those less fortunate than themselves.

It is our strong belief in our country that taxes should be as little as possible, spent as wisely as possible- since it is our money being spent for other things for the greater good.

If I remember right, the current tax code makes up about 80,000 pages.

Think it's about time for some reform?

Reform does not mean we don't pay taxes, but simply getting the code to be more manageable for the common person, getting it more transparent and simpler, leveling the burden of taxes being paid fairly through elimination of deductions and credits, and after all is said and done- making sure that all people have a piece of the burden that is representative of their active role in our Country.

Conservatives believe in lowering the tax burden, and in using those monies efficiently. We need Government to do things for us that we cannot do for ourselves. We do not need Government to be burdensome, overreach their authority, overtax us and spend that wastefully.

Our world has changed significantly since the tax code was started. We are a more global world. We are much more service reliant and have lost manufacturing competitively. The internet allows us to buy and sell without leaving our home anywhere in the world.

The current tax code makes for an unfair landscape of winners and losers, while simultaneously being outdated in getting revenues to government to be spent responsibly.

Concerning taxes, less is more-but starts with reform to level the field for all.

Pro Entitlement Reform

The bulk of the national budget is spent on a few extremely large programs. Regardless of the merits (or lack thereof) of the program, we believe that these programs are in desperate need of reform. They are cumbersome, burdensome, and against our belief in a smaller Government. Entitlements should not be designed or legislated to be ever-growing and all inclusive. The nature of entitlements is to be a safety net for the less fortunate, for those truly incapable of taking care of themselves, and not something that is a Right or Common Expectation for the mass population. Reform, and education of the mass population, is necessary both for financial concerns and cultural benefit.

We all want to pay less taxes, but none of us wants to give up anything. Sound familiar?

Here is the problem- the Math does not Work.

Over decades we have made government larger and larger- Medicare, Medicare, Social Security, and the newly passed Affordable HealthCare Act. Over the course of generations, we have learned to live longer via scientific breakthroughs and nutritional advances. We have improved most aspects of life, yet we have not adjusted our social service programs along the way.

The time is now for Entitlement Reform.

We are currently burdened by 87 Trillion Dollars of Unfunded Liabilities.
We are currently burdened by 16.3 Trillion Dollars of National Debt.

We are currently burdened by 1.5 Trillion Dollars of Budget Deficit each year.
We are currently growing Entitlements at the rate of approximately 8% annually.

The pace of growth and size of debt will break our Country.

Protect the Country by giving up a little now OR Keep "your piece of the pie" and get nothing.

What is YOUR choice?

IF you believe in a smaller efficient compassionate government, then you agree reform is overdue.
IF you don't care about the size of government, then the question is different.

What would YOU do to fix it?

The simple truth is that it cannot continue without change. Do you remember the old Midas commercial?

"You can pay me now or pay me later".

The choice isn't going to be without pain, but sometimes we need to take our medicine to build for a better day in the future.

Our leaders need to come up with fair & balanced answers to lower the threat Entitlements failing.

Pro-States Rights

We believe in a strong nation of states, and that a large cumbersome Federal Government is both restrictive and wasteful. States are empowered to respond to their constituents faster and more efficiently. They are more able to create an environment that represents their people overall, and if someone chooses a different lifestyle- can go to another state where that is better represented. The Federal government over-reach mandates for all states, and therefore creates a culture of "take-it-or-leave it" as citizens cannot move out from under this national policy. This is both contrary to what we believe our Founders intended, unnecessary, and against the grain of a Government that is small and working for "We, the People". The strength of our Nation is empowered individuals make State-wide decisions, and through those two strengths creating a resilient, vibrant and successful United States of America.

Are you a Conservative?

Conservatives believe in the simple truth that the burden of government and the price of unintended consequences, for no extra gain, should be as limited as possible. It is also true that, from our founding days up to current times, the States were designed to be the better level of Government.

Individuals have a greater voice in their State as opposed to the Federal level.

Money collected could be more closely watched and efficiently spent at State level.

The empowerment of individuals is a core trademark of Conservative principles. We need to expand that Freedom, and get large Government out of the way.

When was the last time Government did something well? That it spent money wisely? That is was held accountable to the same standards as your business or home, to simply balance its budget or to live within its means.

If you don't like a State decision, you could always pick any other state (and that competition is wonderfully efficient).

But if you don't like a Federal decision, what are your options? Quit on America?

If States controlled Education, how much better off would our children be?

If the Federal Government and its inherent waste were scaled back, how much money would we save?

Would you rather have a soft bloated Government you can't see or speak out in OR a smaller efficient compassionate Government that encourages you to speak out and is transparent?

The choice is yours. But the reasoning is simple, true, and convincing.

And that, is "WHY?! Go Conservative".

AUTHOR PAGE

John A. Jensen is a proud husband and father of two great children. His previous works include the political book "FixTheNation.com" and the fictional thriller "The Art of Assassination". As a weekly radio talk show host, author, and founder of FixTheNation.com- he is much more interested on Solutions to our Problems, than in the Blame of who has failed America. He lives privately and passionately on Long Island, New York.

The Art of Assassination   (FICTION)
FixTheNation.com   (POLITICS)
            available via Amazon.com

Website-   http://www.FixTheNation.com
Email-   suggestionbox@fixthenation.com

Facebook via http://www.facebook.com/FixTheNation
Twitter via   http://www.twitter.com/FixTheNation

Radio Host @ http://www.blogtalkradio.com/fixthenation

Also: Red State Talk Radio Network
            http://redstatetalkradio.com/
Stitcher.com (News/Politics, Conservative Politics)
http://app.stitcher.com/#browse/23/890482/24053/info
I-Tunes   (Free Download Subscription)

**If you truly enjoyed "Why?! Go Conservative", then I recommend "FixTheNation.com".
**It is also suggested you return to Amazon.com book page to FB 'Like' and Review it.